Small Book With a **Big** Idea

Sara Ting

5 Minute Training to Empower You and Transform Our World

Dedication

This book is dedicated to the human race and to inspiring and empowering humanity to embrace everyone like the sun.

Small Book with a Big Idea
5 Minute Training to Empower You and Transform Our World

This book is offered to you with a deep understanding that you have gifts, talents, and life experiences that make you who you are. Because there is no other human being like you, you have something special to offer the world.

This 5 minute training is about empowering you to live, learn, and work in a world of differences. Every day you're engaged with the diversity of life. Every day there's an opportunity for you to shine and bring light to others.

In my passion and commitment to diversity and inclusion, I've come to understand that at our deepest core each of us wants to be heard, to be valued, to belong, and to give. When we experience this personally and professionally, we can grow in ways we never imagined. We can exceed our own expectations and give our talent and best self to our community and the world.

The impact of not accepting differences…

The devastating impact of not accepting differences was poignantly captured for me in a quote by **Mother Teresa: "I have come more and more to realize that it is being unwanted that is the worst disease that any human being can ever experience."**

What has led me here?

Since 1985, I've been passionately engaged with the issues of diversity and equality as a community activist, TV reporter, educator, diversity trainer, and president of World Unity, Inc., a non-profit organization dedicated to eliminating all forms of prejudice, bias, and discrimination.

This work has opened me up to my humanity. It's deepened my understanding of **what it means to be human.** Surprisingly, twenty five years of addressing the issues of diversity and equality have led me to design a simple, effective 5 minute training program that can **empower all individuals.**

The success of the 5 minute training is dependent upon…

You! The success of the training is totally in your hands. You may find it hard to believe, but the training I will introduce only takes 5 minutes or less.

It can be used every day. You will determine how much you want out of it—how much you want to **stretch your mind and heart.**

What are the benefits of this training and what's in it for you?

For starters, none of us can escape the diversity in humanity. It surrounds us the minute we wake up and engage with life. The benefits to you personally and professionally are invaluable and can **serve you for the rest of your life.**

Engaging with diversity is an endless journey with no end point. The rewards are enriching and priceless.

You discover more of you!

The training has the ability to push buttons.

Be prepared. You might initially think the training is challenging you. If you find yourself having a strong emotional response, a button has been pushed. Don't stop the experience. Keep moving through the feelings.

The stronger the response, the more powerful the breakthrough—and the greater the opportunity for **self-discovery**.

Letting go of some of our pride

A healthy dose of pride isn't bad. We all have some. However, don't let your pride stop you from learning, growing, and finding peace and happiness.

Let your pride welcome this simple 5 minute training. It can develop **new self-awareness** and open up **new possibilities.**

Letting go of the ego

This is a big one. If you let go of your ego, you may receive a powerful response.

You may have a transformative experience.

Don't let your ego get in the way of your experience and the wonderful insight you may receive.

Don't be fooled by the simplicity of the training.

Simple truths in life have always been with us since the beginning of time—truths such as "do unto others as you would have them do unto you" or "the more you give, the more you receive."

If you ponder this training and put it into action, you may see its wisdom and how it can enrich and empower your life.

Some of the many responses to the training

Powerful!
Awesome!
Uplifting
It opened my mind.
Created new awareness
It humbled me.
Evoked tears
I learned I had to forgive.
Everyone should read it.

Keep the mind open like the sky.

As you open your mind to the simple, 5 minute training, be prepared to see how the mind responds and the insights it may offer you.

Be fully present.

Be with yourself,
no distractions,
nothing demanding
or pulling your attention;
allow yourself to fully
experience the 5 minute training.

Put aside skepticism for a moment to invest 5 minutes in you.

There may still be some doubt, but, on the other hand, curiosity as well.

If something takes 5 minutes or less, what do you have to lose?

Listen

Listen to the thoughts and feelings that come up.

You have an opportunity for new self-awareness.

Keep in mind that you are special and there is no one like you.

Be prepared to receive...

New awareness that may transform the way you engage with differences.

To quote Oliver Wendell Holmes,

"A mind stretched by a new idea can never regain its original dimension."

Now, if you're ready, the training begins.

Instructions

Carefully absorb and ponder each word on the following pages.

Be aware of the images, thoughts, and feelings that come up for you.

If there's any resistance, ask yourself why.

Don't skip a page or jump ahead.

Feel free to note your thoughts on the page and date it.

Are you greater than the sun

that shines on everyone:

Black,

Brown,

Yellow,

Red,

And

White

The sun does not discriminate.©

These four simple lines invite you to think about the sun and how inclusive it is of humanity.

The sun embraces everyone, no matter the color of your skin, if you're a man or a woman, old or young, rich or poor, Christian or Muslim, educated or uneducated, gay or straight, physically challenged or not, tall or short, wide or thin, attractive or plain, famous or unknown, strong or weak…the list is endless. It includes people around the world and future generations.

The sun does not exclude you or anyone else. Everyone counts in the eyes of the sun.

**Imagine if you were as inclusive
as the sun,
how empowered you would feel.**

The 5 minute training is over.

Some more engaging thoughts:

You can be who you are under the sun.

In the sunlight, your thoughts, values, beliefs, ideas, and creativity are accepted

We all receive the light.

Even your emotions are completely accepted by
the sun.

If you're happy, joyful, sad, depressed or angry the
sun will still shine on you.

Under the sun, all your feelings receive the light.
No one's feelings are rejected by the sun.

All of your humanity is embraced by the sun,

even that which is invisible.

As you ponder the four lines, think about how you feel about your race and your culture.

Facing our feelings toward our race and culture is very liberating. It freed me up to speak about discrimination and biases. I can remember the moment I discovered my own biases. It was over thirty years ago. I asked myself: *How do I know people reject me because I am Asian?* The answer that came to me was quite surprising. It's poignantly conveyed in this poem:

As I walk down the street
I see rows of white faces
With round eyes
These eyes march by me
And stare straight ahead
No acknowledgement
Of my humanness
Am I invisible
No response
To my smile
Am I ugly

No response
To my hello
Have I done something wrong
Oh no I forgot my eyes are slanted
Friends tell me I'm too sensitive
I shouldn't assume some people
Look at me with racist eyes
How do I know they're rejecting me
Because I'm Asian
I know because
I've rejected Asians too!

"The Sun" poem we used as training has a personal message for each of us.

Ponder the poem, go deep inside, and listen to your inner voice.

Let each page of the book bring light to your thoughts and feelings.

Remember that you have something special to offer the world:

It's buried inside of you.

Extraordinary stories of "The Sun" poem

Over the years, individuals have shared powerful stories of how "The Sun" poem affected them. These stories helped me realize the transformative power of this simple poem.

One individual felt initially challenged by the poem. She thought it said, "Who do you think you are?" She couldn't believe it was speaking to her in this way. To her credit, she read it a second time and that's when the transformation took place—she was humbled.

Another young lady had a profound revelation. Upon first reading it, she hated the poem. A four-by-eight-foot graphic design of it was hanging in the YWCA because their first imperative is the elimination of racism. She could not ignore the poem. Every time she walked into the lobby, these four lines silently spoke to her. They managed to open up a heart scarred by painful memories of discrimination growing up in Boston as an

Asian-American woman. It wasn't until seeing the poem several times as she entered the lobby that she came to a profound realization—she had to let go of the past, and learn to forgive.

What is one of the greatest gifts you'll discover?

You may laugh at what I'm about to tell you. If you're able to have the humility and self-awareness to admit that you have some biases, guess what you just discovered? You're human! Welcome to the human race! Welcome to humanity!

All human beings have biases. None of us are free of them.

Inanimate objects have no biases: The chair in which you sit, the floor on which you walk, the bed in which you sleep have no biases and will accept anyone. Human beings will have theirs, some big ones and some small ones.

It is a great gift to embrace your humanity

and challenge your ways of thinking

Consider this...

Every day you go through a daily ritual to be clean. You brush your teeth, wash your face, and take a shower.

Imagine what you would look like if you didn't clean for a month? Not a pretty picture.

What are you doing every day to clear your mind and prepare it for a new day? What are you doing to wash off any small inequities, assumptions, unconscious biases, or negative experiences that may still be festering in your mind?

Imagine what your mind might look like and how it would function if you didn't clean it for a month? Could your mind be totally focused on the present, free of assumptions and unconscious biases?

Are you sure there's not something buried in there from a year ago or longer that is still waiting to be resolved, healed, or let go?

Imagine clearing your mind every day by pondering "The Sun" poem.

What are some of the benefits of pondering this poem every day?

Deepen your understanding of inclusion

Deepen your understanding of diversity

Deepen your understanding of leadership

Become more empowered

Expand your creative spirit

Become more self-aware

Experience life in a new way

See new opportunities in life

Experience your professional environment
in a new way

See your colleagues in a new way

Experience conversations in a new way

Widen your circle of friends

Receive unexpected gifts from life

Receive unexpected surprises

Develop more compassion

The list is endless…

There is a guarantee
with this training.

We've all heard of two guarantees in life: death and taxes. This training offers you another one. I guarantee between now and the day you leave this earth, as you practice this 5 minute training you'll still make mistakes in your efforts to accept and respect people's differences—some small and some big. When you make them, does it make you a terrible person? Does it mean you're a racist, sexist, and all the other labels we give each other when we make a mistake? No, it only means you're human.

Can you be as accepting of your mistakes and others as the sun? Does the sun label us when we make a mistake?

Transform yourself.

If, by the end of the 5 minute training, you discover something new about yourself, it may be the starting point of a great transformation. The more you reflect on "The Sun" poem, the more you may discover.

The more you let go, the more you will receive.

Challenge yourself.

As you reflect on "The Sun" poem each day,

can you

be like the sun and bring light to every situation?

The power of choice

This training is in your hands.

Remember: It takes less than 5 minutes.

You have the choice to reflect on "The Sun" poem once a day, a week, a month, or a year.

It can empower you in ways you may never imagine.

There are endless possibilities for new insights, new self-awareness, and new ways to engage with life and give the best of **YOU!**

The power of poetry in Nelson Mandela's life...

Nelson Mandela was imprisoned for twenty-seven years for taking a stand for equality in South Africa. The poem "Invictus" empowered him to live through the suffering and pain he endured in prison.

INVICTUS

Out of the night that covers me,
Black as the Pit from pole to pole,
I thank whatever gods may be
For my unconquerable soul.

In the fell clutch of circumstance
I have not winced nor cried aloud.
Under the bludgeonings of chance
My head is bloody, but unbowed.

Beyond this place of wrath and tears
Looms but the Horror of the shade,

And yet the menace of the years
Finds, and shall find, me unafraid.

It matters not how strait the gate,
How charged with punishments the scroll.
I am the master of my fate:
I am the captain of my soul.

—William Ernest Henley

Embracing diversity is an endless journey.

"Invictus" empowered Nelson Mandela to endure twenty-seven years in prison. While we're free to live in America, we can be held captive in a different way. We can be imprisoned by our fears, ego, pride, our past and our unconscious biases which can keep us from connecting with someone who's different and being fully present.

If we reflect on "The Sun" poem every day, it can free us to be present to each other's humanity and be empowered every day to engage with life.

Dare to be as great as the sun.

Dare to shine on everyone.

The sun gives to us all the time and never receives anything in return. It's a great teacher of humility and gratitude.

Transforming the world begins with a thought…planting a new thought is like planting a new seed.

Between 2007 and 2009, "The Sun" poem was planted in every state in America in educational institutions. It can be seen on colorful posters, bookmarks, or magnets. One teacher in Kentucky who introduced the poem to her students through bookmarks said, "I'm excited about what 'The Sun' poem can do for our school, our community, and, on that basis, for the world" (Evelyn Nichols).

If you want to grow a new garden,
you plant new seeds.
If you want to create a new world,
we need to plant new thoughts.

Albert Einstein once said, "You can never solve a problem at the same level of consciousness that created it. You must stand on a higher ground."

The Sun poem creates a new awareness. The more self-aware you are the more possibilities you will see and new doors will open up.

Power in numbers

Imagine if one million people read this poem, reflected on its meaning, passed it along, and, through citizens, "The Sun" poem was planted in towns, cities, and countries around the world.

You and I have the opportunity to transform the world, to empower individuals and leaders to look at differences through the eyes of the sun by sharing "The Sun" poem:

Are you greater than the sun

that shines on everyone:

Black, Brown, Yellow, Red and White?

The sun does not discriminate. ©

Every day we have an opportunity to shine and be as great as the sun.
We have the opportunity to help transform the world.

Gratitude

I thank you for investing your money and time in reading this *Small Book with a Big Idea*. I thank the sun for giving us life and inspiring me every day to be bright, inclusive, humble, compassionate, and forgiving. And I thank God, my creator for giving me life.

Family

I thank my mother and father for their love, support, dedication to the family and choosing to live in America one of the greatest countries in the world. Their upbringing in China helped me understand and appreciate the challenges of growing up in a multicultural world. I thank my siblings, Stephen, Simeon, Sharon and Sandee for their love and support. Growing up with them has deepened my understanding of diversity. And to my in-laws, Peter, Li-Hsi, and Andre, I thank them for who they are and the diversity they bring to my life and our family. I thank all of my nieces and nephews for the joy they've brought to my life: Arielle, Alexis, Ryan, Derek, Erin, and Lara. Each is so different—each precious and special.

Friends and Colleagues

I thank all the students and teachers with whom I have worked for over twenty years, who helped me stay connected to my humanity, and inspired me to keep teaching the art of writing poetry.

I thank all the trustees, board of directors, advisors, volunteers, contributors, and supporters of World Unity, Inc. for continuing to deepen my understanding of the issue of differences, and for empowering me in my passion to promote diversity and inclusion and to fulfill my mission to build a landmark to promote diversity and inclusion.

I thank all of my friends, colleagues, and supporters, of diverse backgrounds, who have accepted me, recognized me, touched my life, and helped me become the person I am today: Michael, Trish, Delores, Wendy, Nancy, Maria, Lily, Elaine, Lillian, David, Jim, Peter, George, Bob, Judith, Howard, Joel, Anowsh, Phil, John, Russell, Thomas, Tom, Jim, Keith, Brad, Lauren, Cherie, Susan, Lloyd, Karoline, Burt, Adita, Raul, Sandra, Amit, Jan, Frank, Phillip,

Larry, Tracy, Barbara, Rose Anne, Beth, Amy, Ted, Sarah, Fran, Albert, Clark, Patrick, Billy, Patricia, Stephanie, Joanne, Richard, Carlton, Shakeh, Bill, Judy, Robert, Dave, Billie, Yoke, Ed, Tony, Brian, Seth, Karl, Tasos, Stephen, Tiffany, Christine, Shau, Herb, D.E. Dale, Bruce, Leslie, Jackie, Valerie, Julie, Alberto, Kate, Scott, K.T., Liz, Juan, Apolo, Vincent, Doreen, Donna, Jim, Oz, Don, Harriet, Pablo, Charlie, Felix, Roger, May, Joe, San San, Colleen, Rob, Misha, Brenda, Bahman, Karen, Linda, Fran, Adnelly, Chris, Ann, Ramona, Marjorie, Yvonne, Laura, Paul, Deborah, Anthony, Sam, Jeff, Steven, Shane, Sharon, Colette, Milton, Stephen, Ron, Clark, Patrick, Aidee, Laila, Cameron, Pablo, Vivian, Richard, Jeff, Lisa, Trinh, Darnell, Nat, Jana, Julius, Ryan, Giewee, JoAnn, Meghan, Lauren, Cora, Ashley, Katie, Liz, Lisa, Rebecca, Melissa, Lesley, Ayo, Lorna, Mary, Lori, Taline, Deborah, Jen, Janet, Sabrina, Aloysius, Helen, Chris, Deanna, Anna, Robin, Ken, Eleanor, Jesenia, Mark, Kennilyn, Kimberly, Tammy, Evelyn, Erica, Bobby, Art, Laura, Daveta, Ramon, Eduardo, Julia, Glen, Herman, Lashasa, Jose, Justin, Rodney, Marva, Kermit, Jamie, Ricardo, Christina, Johnnie, Rose, Lucy, Kelly, CJ, Erin, Cecil, Kimberly, Alan, Vernon, Hugh, Valerie, Richard, Joyce, Charles, Vicky, Drena, Roberto, Kassandra, Sheryl, June, Shelly, Martin, William, Jamie, Carl, Rose, Wanda, Kurt, Ola, Richard, Gina, Tim, Janet, Pam, Cheryl, Elizabeth, Jill, Matthew, Malika, Beatrice, Dottie, Ronnie, Diane, Fay, Ebi, Gordon, Raj, Craig, Carmen, Doris, Antonio, Gayle, Dyango, Victoria and Timothy.

Bio

Sara Ting is the daughter of a former diplomat with the Nationalist Chinese government. She's the oldest daughter and one of five children. Her passion for diversity and inclusion led her to community activism, TV reporting, diversity training, and teaching students the art of writing poetry. Since 1985, she has been designing and presenting diversity and inclusion programs to schools, colleges, city and state agencies, companies, and non-profit organizations throughout Massachusetts. In 2007, she introduced a diversity tool to schools across the country. In a little over twenty-four months, the tool was in educational institutions in every state.

In 1993, Sara founded World Unity, Inc., a non-profit organization dedicated to making a continuing and lasting contribution toward the elimination of all forms of prejudice, bias, and discrimination. This mission will be achieved through the creation of a permanent landmark showcasing "The Sun" poem. It will be built in Children's Wharf Park in the Seaport District of Boston.

Sara is a graduate of Boston University, School of Fine and Applied Arts.

Ms. Ting is available for speaking engagements and presenting workshops. For more information visit: www.asthesun.com

To learn about the World Unity Landmark, visit: www.worldunityinc.org